Dec 2017

First Drawings

Cars and Trucks

BIG BUDDY
FIRST DRAWINGS
BOOKS

Big Buddy Books
An Imprint of Abdo Publishing
abdopublishing.com

By Katie Lajiness

abdopublishing.com

Printed in the United States of America, North Mankato, Minnesota.
092016
012017

THIS BOOK CONTAINS
RECYCLED MATERIALS

Illustrations: Michael Jacobsen/Spectrum Studio
Interior Photos: Deposit Photos

Coordinating Series Editor: Tamara L. Britton
Graphic Design: Taylor Higgins, Maria Hosley

Publisher's Cataloging-in-Publication Data

Names: Lajiness, Katie, author.
Title: Cars and trucks / by Katie Lajiness.
Description: Minneapolis, MN : Abdo Publishing, 2017. | Series: First drawings |
Includes index.
Identifiers: LCCN 2016945187 | ISBN 9781680785203 (lib. bdg.) |
ISBN 9781680798807 (ebook)
Subjects: LCSH: Automobiles in art--Juvenile literature. | Trucks in art--
Juvenile literature. | Drawing--Technique--Juvenile literature.
Classification: DDC 743.8/96292--dc23
LC record available at http://lccn.loc.gov/2016945187

Table of Contents

BASIC SHAPES

Circle | Oval | Rectangle | Square | Triangle

getting started

Today, you're going to draw cars and trucks. Not sure you know how to draw? Cars and trucks are easy to **sketch** if you break them down into circles, ovals, rectangles, squares, and triangles.

To begin, you'll need paper, a sharpened pencil, a big eraser, and a flat surface. Draw each shape lightly. When these **guidelines** are light, it is easy to erase and try again.

BASIC SHAPES

Volkswagen Beetle

Dump Truck

Monster Truck

Race Car

Semitruck

Adding color

Once you learn to draw an object, you may want to add color. Let's learn how to mix colors and add shading.

Shading

MARKERS
Use similar colors to create shading.

PENCILS AND CRAYONS
Use less pressure for lighter shades and more pressure for darker shades.

PAINTS
Add white to lighten and black or blue to darken shades.

There are three primary colors. They are red, yellow, and blue. These colors cannot be made by mixing other colors. However, you can make many colors by mixing primary colors together.

Color mixing

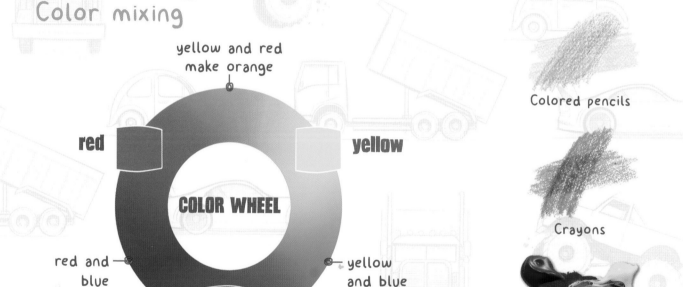

yellow and red make orange

red

yellow

COLOR WHEEL

red and blue make purple

yellow and blue make green

blue

Colored pencils

Crayons

Paints

Tip Create **contrast** by using colors from opposite ends of the color wheel.

Let's learn to draw a Beetle!

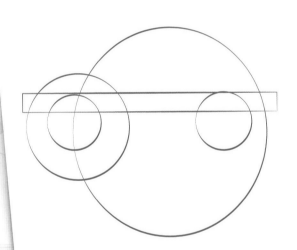

STEP 1

Draw basic circle and rectangle **guidelines** for the body and tires.

Erase guidelines
once you have
the parts drawn.

STEP **2**

Connect the shapes to form the car's **outline**.

STEP **3**

Sketch light **guidelines** for the windows, door, and wheels.

Erase guidelines once you have the parts drawn.

STEP 4

Now add **details** by filling in the car's door, door handle, windows, wheel wells, and rear light.

STEP 5

Create **texture** and shape by adding shading.

It's time for some color! You can add your own color and shading to personalize your drawing.

YOU DID IT!

Bravo! You drew a Beetle.

Dump Truck

Let's learn to draw a dump truck!

STEP 1

Draw basic square, rectangle, and circle **guidelines** for the body, dump bed, and tires.

Erase guidelines
once you have
the parts drawn.

STEP 2

Connect the shapes to form the
dump truck's **outline**.

STEP 3

Draw in windows. Add **details** to
the body and wheel.

STEP 4

Now add **details** to the dump bed. Draw a door handle, rearview mirror, and back tires fender.

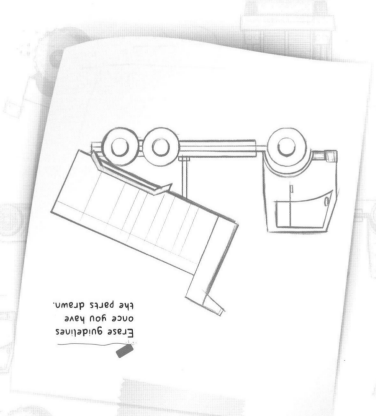

Erase guidelines once you have the parts drawn.

STEP 5

Create **texture** and shape by adding shading.

It's time for some color!
You can add your own
color and shading to
personalize your drawing.

YOU DID IT!

Well done! You
drew a dump truck.

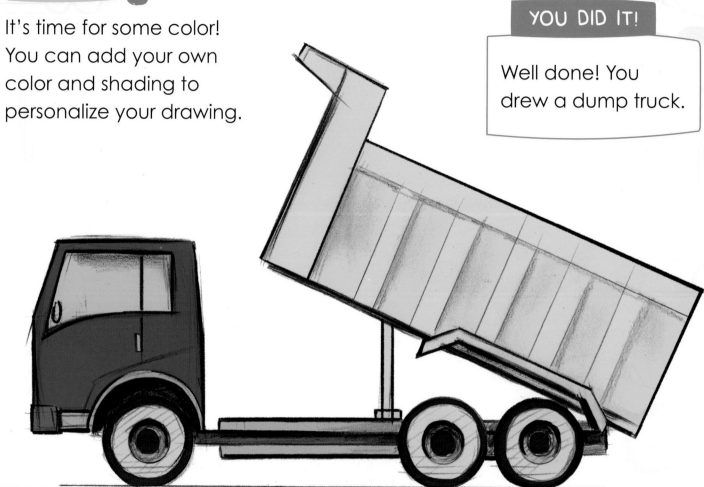

Monster Truck

Let's learn to draw a
monster truck!

Draw basic rectangle and circle
guidelines for the body, cab,
and tires.

Erase guidelines
once you have
the parts drawn.

STEP 2

Connect the shapes to form the truck's **outline**. Add **details** to your tires.

STEP 3

Sketch guidelines to add **depth** to your monster truck. Draw in windows, another set of wheels, and add roll bars to the truck bed.

STEP 4

Now add **details** to the truck's underbody. Add a flag to the back.

STEP 5

Create **texture** and shape by adding shading to your monster truck.

It's time for some color! You can add your own color and shading to personalize your drawing.

Congratulations! You drew a monster truck.

19

Race Car

Let's learn to draw a race car!

Draw basic rectangle and circle **guidelines** for the body and tires.

Erase guidelines once you have the parts drawn.

STEP 2

Connect the shapes to form the car's **outline**.

STEP 3

Sketch the wheels and window.

STEP 4

Fill in the race car's features such as a window bar, a rear spoiler, and lights.

STEP 5

Create **texture** and shape by adding shading to your race car.

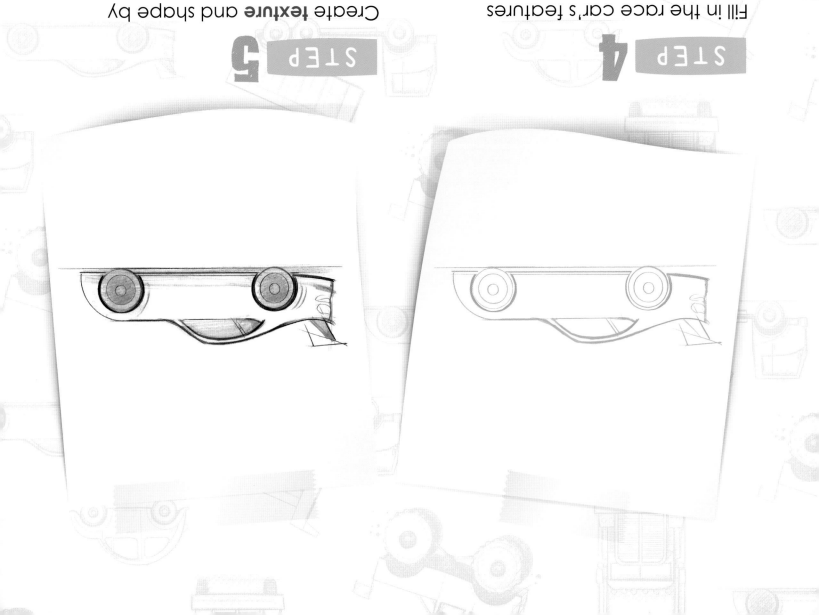

It's time for some color! You can add your own color and shading to personalize your drawing.

Yippee! You drew a race car.

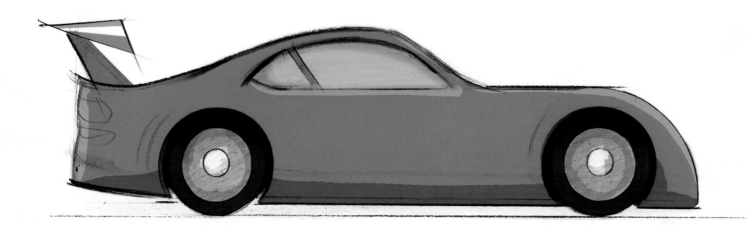

Let's learn to draw a semitruck!

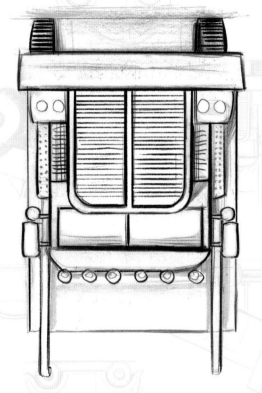

STEP 1

Draw basic rectangles for the body, bumper, and tires. This is the truck's **outline**.

Semitruck

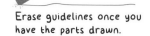

Erase guidelines once you have the parts drawn.

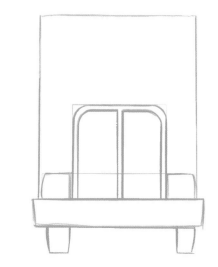

STEP 2

Draw rectangle **guidelines** to build the grille and fenders.

STEP 3

Create rounded edges along the grille and fenders.

STEP 4

Sketch a square and rectangles for the cab and windows of your semitruck.

Erase guidelines once you have the parts drawn.

STEP 5

Continue adding **details**, such as the sun visor. Each new shape creates **depth**.

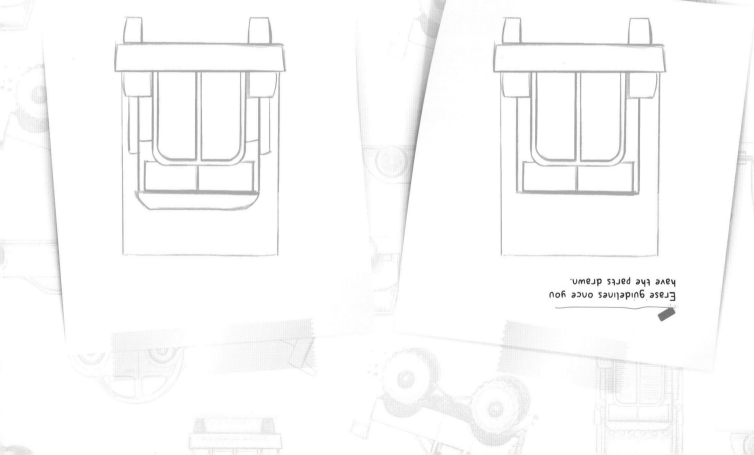

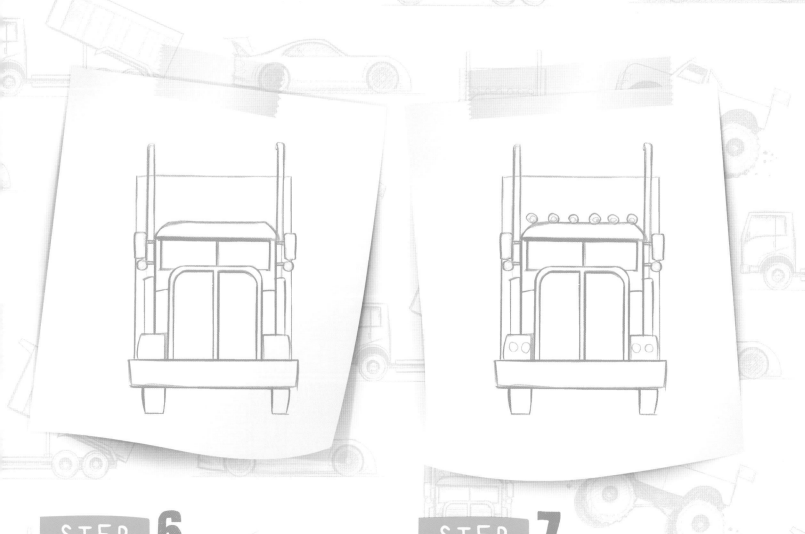

STEP **6**

Fill in the truck's exhaust pipes and mirrors.

STEP **7**

Add the semitruck's lights.

Tools There are many tools you can use to add color such as crayons, colored pencils, paints, or markers.

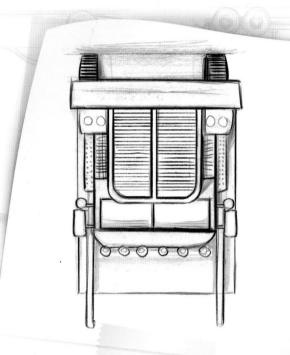

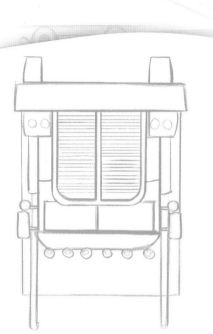

STEP 9

Create **texture** and shape by adding shading.

STEP 8

Add straight lines to create the truck's grille.

It's time for some color! You can add your own color and shading to personalize your drawing.

YOU DID IT!

Yay! You drew a semitruck.

To build your drawing skills, practice finding basic shapes in everyday objects. Finding basic shapes can help you draw almost anything. Use what you've learned to draw other cars and trucks. The more you draw, the better you will be!

Glossary

contrast the amount of difference in color or brightness.

depth measurement from top to bottom or from front to back.

detail a minor decoration, such as a cat's whiskers.

guideline a rule or instruction that shows or tells how something should be done.

outline the outer edges of a shape.

sketch to make a rough drawing.

texture the look or feel of something.

Websites

To learn more about First Drawings, visit **booklinks.abdopublishing.com**.
These links are routinely monitored and updated to provide
the most current information available.

Index